The Human Element

THOMAS CLEARY

The
Human Element

A COURSE IN
RESOURCEFUL THINKING

SHAMBHALA
Boston & London
1996

Shambhala Publications, Inc.
Horticultural Hall
300 Massachusetts Avenue
Boston, Massachusetts 02115

9 8 7 6 5 4 3 2 1
First Paperback Edition

Printed in the United States of America

⊗ This edition is printed on acid-free paper that meets
the American National Standards Institute Z39.48 Standard.

Distributed in the United States by Random House, Inc.,
and in Canada by Random House of Canada Ltd

The Library of Congress catalogues the hardcover edition of this book as follows:

Cleary, Thomas F., 1949–
    The human element: a course in resourceful thinking/
  Thomas Cleary. — 1st ed.
        p.   cm.
    Includes bibliographical references.
    ISBN 0-87773-994-3
    ISBN 1-57062-205-1 (pbk.)
    1. Success. 2. Success in business. 3. Leadership.
  4. Philosophy, Oriental — Quotations, maxims, etc.   I. Title.
  BJ1611.2.C5427   1994   93-37729
  650.1 — dc20   CIP

Contents

The Human Element

INTRODUCTION

If technology is an embodiment of method, or means, management of human resources can be considered a kind of technology.

From this point of view, it becomes important to look at differences between the technology to be used with machines and the technology to be used with human beings.

Simple as this premise may sound, human beings today are unfortunately found all too often resigned to being treated like machines, if for no other reason than that machines are considered as economically important as human beings.

The deceptive notion that this implies a real and necessary antagonism between technology and humanism, however, is a myth that inhibits the full development of both.

The power of machines seems so great in some areas that it can distract attention from the human elements of their operation, which human elements nevertheless grow *not less* but *more* important in proportion to the power of the machines.

Humanistic arguments against technology, and technological arguments against humanism, are both manifestations of a misplacement of emphasis, and a mistaken belief that the relative importance of these aspects of life rise and fall in an inverse proportion to one another.

Historical processes have resulted in the growth of several bodies of literature dealing with the cultivation of sophistication in recognizing, organizing, and developing human resources. In them are materials that can and do perennially stimulate resourceful thinking in people facing challenging and stressful predicaments.

This literature is about the human element of the total world, the human being as the brain of the material, scientific, and technical body of the world. It is about the evolution and development of the human element in the totality of the life of the world, and how the qualities of these processes are reflected in the experience and fulfillment of the individual human being.

The humanistic themes of such advanced educational materials, therefore, are not based upon the misconstrued idea of a fundamental antagonism between humanity and technology. This unnecessarily wasteful idea is just a recast of the self-confirming belief that religion and science are doomed, by the very natures of faith and reason, to oppose one another in some way.

In reality, the historical opposition between religion and science, or between humanism and technocracy, has been in the nature of politics and its congeners, not in the inherent essence of what are in reality like brain and body to one another.

Technology is an important, even dominant, element in life today; no sensible humanism can ignore this empirical fact and still hope to fulfill its humanistic aims and ideals in a practical way. Technology is so influential in the whole world today that it affects even those who have never enjoyed its amenities.

Technology is important today, furthermore, not only for today but also for the fact that it will affect all people in the future, both those who do and those who do not enjoy its amenities. This is why the human element in the application and operation of technology does not decrease but increases in importance with the growth of power and sophistication in the technology.

The development and employment of human resources is therefore of ongoing, increasing, and evolving importance to human society as technology develops and grows ever more powerful.

When the same technology is used in spite of changing conditions, obsolescence and decline take place. Similarly, when the methods and goals of development and employment of human resources are those of a past no longer producing adequate results for the present and future, the human element begins to lose certain abilities.

One of these abilities is the power to move the evolution of technology forward deliberately, effectively, and meaningfully. Under these conditions, with the gradual dilapidation of that faculty formerly known in philosophical parlance as free will, the brain eventually begins to lose the ability to keep up with the natural evolution of technology in the laboratory of competitive human behavior.

It has often been assumed that advanced human sciences were always carried out in special milieus such as monasteries or academies, but in reality they were adapted to all walks of life and all sorts of contingencies over centuries of practical application. To the extent that they were subordinated to personal and political ambitions, nevertheless, the human sciences were overexploited but underused.

Nowadays monasteries and academies are largely equivalent to museums. "First establish a firm foothold in daily activities within society," says *The Secret of the Golden Flower,* a textbook of higher psychology written in China at the time of the American Revolution; "only then can you cultivate realization and understand the essence of mind." This new wave of an ancient ocean of teachings heralded the modern dispensation of the perennial Ways.

In America, where the business community is increasingly being asked to assume roles and responsibilities formerly discharged mainly by families, schools, social communities, and governments, it is becoming increasingly imperative to seek the use of whatever may be available to assist the mutual enhancement of individual and group activity, particularly in such a heterogeneous society. The effort required to make the fullest possible use of such materials, furthermore, has in itself the power to develop precisely the sort of constructive versatility that humanity needs to meet the challenges of the twenty-first century.

One of the ironies of history in respect to the great traditions of advanced education is that the potential of their teachings has been regarded as both a blessing and a threat. Just as there have always been individuals and organizations attempting to use the knowledge transmitted in such traditions for the uplift of self and society, there have also been individuals and organizations attempting to use the same knowledge for personal power and control over other people.

This split in the reception of spiritual tradition has often taken place along social and political lines, resulting in what are known as "court" and "field" versions of knowledge and education. Royal and imperial courts of the old world commonly attempted to manipulate philosophy and religion to use for the purpose of consolidation and aggrandizement of their own political power. Workers in the "field" of society at large, in contrast, were more interested in adapting ancient teachings to the needs of contemporary people, both individually and collectively.

This distinction is of critical importance in understanding the different kinds of influence that traditional educational methodologies actually exert in practice. It is also therefore crucial for distinguishing practical applications of those methodologies for the present and future from those belonging to the past.

One of the most significant differences between court and field studies in higher thought is that between the "court" attempt to construct intellectual systems out of ancient classics and the situational "field" use of tested materials to stimulate practical insight and creative thought, fostering pragmatic applications in contemporary life situations and thereby furthering the development of a fertile and resourceful mind.

The literatures on which this course in resourceful thinking draws originated in the ancient Orient, where enormous accomplishments rested on the wealth of human resources. Most of the works cited, furthermore, have been known in the West for more than a century, some for two or more centuries, if often in crude and culturally biased versions. Not only are these literatures therefore naturalized to some degree in the West, but they are also the object today of increasing attention on the part of

Western people in all walks of life, including many of those for whom ostensibly ancient or Asian thinking had hitherto seemed irrelevant at best. Each of the four sections draws on a major tradition of practical philosophy; after a general introduction to these ways of thought, actual extracts from important traditional textbooks are translated and interpreted for modern audiences, followed by a brief explanatory bibliography of resources for each tradition.

Confucianism

Confucianism of some sort was the orthodox ideology of China for more than two thousand years. In some forms, Confucianism was tremendously influential in Japan, Korea, and Vietnam as well. Nowadays it is widely recognized in the West that certain aspects of Confucianism subtend the outstanding managerial skills shown by noncommunist Chinese, Japanese, and Koreans.

Ironically, one of the main dicta of Confucianism, that profit is a base motive in comparison with duty and justice, would seem to disqualify it as a useful ideology for business, where it has nevertheless flourished in its own way. While literalistic interpretations of the Confucian principle may formerly have led Asian governments into disastrously negligent policies toward commerce, nevertheless, the subordination of profit motive to duty and justice does not actually weaken the practicality of Confucianism in the modern world.

This fact can be observed in the exemplary modern Japanese Matsushita business philosophy, formulated on ancient models by the late Matsushita Kōnosuke, who was popularly known as *Keiei no Kamisan,* or "The Genius of Management." His philosophy is based on the idea that industry and business have a duty to fulfill the needs of society, and that profit is legitimate and indeed necessary in that it operates as a means of fulfilling this duty. From such a point of view, to make a fair profit is itself a just duty insofar as it enables an enterprise to continue to serve the public.

In this sense, profit and duty are no longer at odds but even complement one another. The greater the extent to which an enterprise fulfills its just duty of serving the public, the greater its profits; and the greater its profits, the greater the capacity of the enterprise to produce such goods or perform such services as society deems necessary, useful, or desirable.

This sort of "field" Confucianism has always tended to be far more individualistic, varied, pragmatic, and interesting than "court" Confucianism, which relied heavily on authoritarianism and mechanisms of mind control. Communist totalitarianism in China was in fact an extension of this ancient court tradition, even as it pretended to repudiate the past.

Most of the clichés about Confucianism well known in the West come from "court" Confucianism or impressions thereof. This is a result of specific historical conditions, including the remaining force of the very mind-control mechanisms used by ancient courts.

For the purposes pursued in *The Human Element,* sayings of Confucius himself will be taken to stand for the true pulse of this philosophy and the best of what it has to offer any generation that encounters it.

Taoism

Taoism is a general name for the most ancient body of knowledge in East Asia. Legend connects the origins of civilization in Asia to Taoist giants of remote antiquity. Whereas Western scholars following Chinese court tradition are accustomed to thinking of Taoism as antithetical to Confucianism, orthodox Taoists consider Confucianism to be an offshoot of an originally unified tradition.

The schism of the ancient tradition into Confucian and Taoist specialties occurred during the first half of the first millennium BCE. It was fostered by pressures mounting along the well-established court/field division. This split in Chinese culture and society was like a geological fault along which earthquakes erupted time and again over the ages.

While Confucianism specialized in social and political studies, Taoist interests included natural sciences and higher psychology. Although there were many controversies between extremely polarized factions of Confucians and Taoists, everyone had some exposure to both traditions, and all people in positions of power studied them both. In many cases, however, Taoist studies among Confucians and other secular specialists were kept secret, because the reputation of Taoist adepts for extraordinary powers was dangerous for lay people in public life.

Taoism has often been misrepresented as esoteric and otherworldly because of this secrecy. The political standards of Taoism were so lofty that they exposed despots of China as the tyrants that they were, thus also endangering the lives of those who espoused this philosophy. When Confucianism was formally declared the sole orthodox way of thought by the Chinese government in the second century BCE, the main stream of Taoism went underground until the collapse of the dynasty hundreds of years later.

Taoism reemerged from its privacy into public and political life near the end of the second century CE with unprecedented power. A secret revolutionary organization led by Taoist healers spread widely through the countryside, awaiting the moment to overthrow a corrupt and oppressive regime that had been controlling China and Korea for nearly four hundred years.

Although this movement was betrayed by a traitor and lost its military edge, the shattering force of its residual power played a critical part in the downfall of the dynasty and the rebirth of a new China. For a time there was even a separate Taoist state with diplomatic recognition from the Chinese government.

After the breakup of the Chinese empire in the third century CE, Taoism played several roles in society. Many Chinese Confucian intellectuals, no longer required to maintain the narrow views of the orthodox school of thought, plunged into the broader traditions of Taoism. These thinkers produced vigorous movement in literature and the arts, celebrating a new, more expansive consciousness.

During this period large areas of the old Chinese empire were reconquered or taken anew by smaller nations to the north and west. This political situation allowed for a major influx of shamanistic and Buddhist ideas and practices into China. Taoism played a significant role in absorbing and adapting new currents of thought, developing new institutions and creating new literature to accommodate intellectual and cultural changes.

After China was reunited near the end of the sixth cen-

tury, Taoism briefly moved to center stage under the re-
splendent T'ang dynasty (619–905), whose culture amal-
gamated the results of centuries of international
exchange. For a time the Taoist classics were granted the
stamp of orthodoxy, and it became possible to qualify for
civil service by taking a degree in Taoist studies.

The new official acceptance of Taoism resulted in numerous important findings in researches on ancient Taoism. Less positive was the influence of orthodoxy on the
court/field division in Taoist studies. While Taoist
churches expanded and Taoist liturgy and literature grew
to colossal proportions under royal patronage, the spiritual interest in Taoism drifted away from this formalism.
By the end of the T'ang dynasty a new Taoist movement
was already emerging in the field, returning to the original principles and practices of ancient Taoism.

After the end of the T'ang dynasty, the next major
phase in the development of Chinese culture was the
Sung dynasty (960–1278). During the Sung dynasty lively
new schools of Confucianism and Taoism emerged with
resounding force, championing the ancient classics yet
creating radical changes in their exegetical traditions.
While these cultural events have puzzled many scholars
looking only at Confucianism, there is undeniable evidence that the Sung dynasty revivals of Taoism and Con-

fucianism were both directly stimulated and informed by Ch'an Buddhism.

In spite of its great cultural achievements, Sung dynasty China was ultimately ruined by militarism and overrun by a series of conquerors, culminating in the occupation of the entire country by a dynasty of Mongolian warriors. Although curious and fairly tolerant of different ways of thought, the Mongolian Khans were wary of the political power of organized religion. They destroyed most of the Taoist canon and controlled the Confucians by establishing a radically circumscribed curriculum for the civil service examination system.

These circumstances naturally aggravated the court/field split in both Taoism and Confucianism, with much of the serious spiritual and intellectual activity going underground. In some cases this underground cultural activity was also linked to grass roots liberation movements.

When the Mongolian Khanate was driven from China by the native Ming dynasty in the fourteenth century, the new government repressed these movements as severely as had the Mongols. Far from liberating China from the repressive rule of the Mongolian Khans, the new Ming dynasty focused most of its attention on preserving its own power.

The Ming government continued attempts to control

thought, suppressing Buddhism and Taoism and adopting the Khans' measures to restrict the Confucian intelligentsia to a narrow and permanently fixed curriculum. The Manchu Ch'ing dynasty that took over China from the Ming dynasty in the seventeenth century continued these mind-control policies for another three hundred years, all the way into the early twentieth century, leaving an indelible impression on orthodox scholarship in China.

Throughout this difficult history, however, there have always been those who approached the classics without political ambitions but rather for their own personal development, for the improvement of their familial, social, and professional conduct and relationships, for the education and welfare of their communities, and for a sense of connection with a greater reality.

The Book of Change

The *I Ching,* or *The Book of Change,* is one of the oldest and most popular books in the world. Although it is a most ancient sourcebook of both Confucianism and Taoism, antedating both the *Analects* of Confucius and the *Tao Te Ching* of the Taoist ancestor Lao-tzu, *The Book of Change* by itself is so cryptic that these later philosophies are traditionally used to decode it.

The Book of Change in the general form it is known today is approximately three thousand years old. It is the third in a series of such texts, its antecessors supposed by some scholars to have been composed six and twelve hundred years earlier. All three of these *Change* books were associated with the founding of ancient dynasties, whose early kings were tutored by Taoist sages.

The last and most refined of the books of *Change,* which is still in use today, is attributed to the founders of the Chou dynasty, who lived in the twelfth and eleventh centuries BCE. These founders, however, were themselves students of a Taoist of towering intellect and colossal knowledge, whose mastery included political and tactical sciences. It is entirely probable, therefore, that *The Book of Change* should really be attributed to the teacher of its reputed authors.

Considered the most profound of the Chinese classics, *The Book of Change* has been interpreted in many different ways, according to each of various schools of thought. Although it has a standard form as a book, there are also numerous traditional systems used for restructuring and reorganizing elements of *The Book of Change* in order to bring out its otherwise hidden dimensions.

Teachings on the Art of War

Because of the attention devoted to social sciences by classical Chinese thinkers, philosophies of conflict and crisis management naturally developed in parallel with the organizational concepts and techniques on which the early successes of civilization were based.

Works on political and military strategy have been traced back to the twelfth century BCE, when the original knowledge subtending Taoism, Confucianism, and *The Book of Change* was still preserved in a comprehensive and unified tradition rather than specialized into distinct branches. Focus on political and military strategy naturally sharpened with the decay of the classical Chinese social order from the eighth through the third centuries BCE, but the art of war nevertheless remained embedded in one or another framework of broader human science.

Probably the best-known classic on strategic arts is Sun-tzu's *Art of War,* followed by the anonymous mnemonic work *Thirty-six Strategies.* The former text has been known in the West for more than two hundred years and has been translated into several European languages. Both classics have gained widespread attention in the West in recent years. As in their native culture, what is more, both works are understood to relate to other human activities and concerns besides war in a literal sense.

The main difference still existing between Eastern and Western studies of *The Art of War* is that many Westerners omit parallel study of Taoism, Confucianism, and the *I Ching.* This is something unthinkable in the East; it may gradually disappear in the West.

It is for this reason that extracts from *The Art of War* and *Thirty-six Strategies* are included in this workbook in spite of their apparent incongruity. Avoidance of incongruity, both conscious and subconscious, is a universal mental habit that is, unfortunately, regularly targeted for exploitation in strategic warfare. The ability to entertain very different views of reality without mutual interference is therefore not only an avenue to higher intellectual ability but also a prime method of self-defense against the vulnerabilities caused by ignorance, blindness, and sentimental prejudice.

Again, because the commentary throughout the book is intended to stimulate thought rather than delimit meaning, the methodology of the commentary on extracts from *The Art of War* and *Thirty-six Strategies* includes deliberate provocation and radical disillusion. The purpose of this, as with all the commentary in the book, is to extend the horizon of perception and thought by illustrating insights and ideas triggered by contact with perennial observations and ideas.

Confucius

* * *

On listening

> Confucius said, "Don't promote people just because of what they say. Don't ignore something that is said just because of who says it."

One reason people shouldn't be promoted just because of what they say is that they may be parroting the ideas of others. And yet this is also a reason not to ignore something said just because of who says it. The unifying thread is to focus on ideas rather than personalities.

* * *
* *

Conventions

> Confucius said, "When everyone dislikes something, examine it. When everyone likes something, examine it."

Spontaneous unanimity is a rare phenomenon. Induced unanimity can conceal latent contradictions and oppositions that may fester and erupt in time. Unanimity may not be the result of an inherent property of the object but may be a result of the desire for confirmation and assurance overriding differences of perception and opinion.

This can turn into an indiscriminate blindness that can be very dangerous; and so both Confucianism and Taoism recommend that when everyone likes or dislikes something, the astute observer should look for the presence of conditioning factors and influences outside the object of approval or disapproval itself. In this way a more objective understanding of the total phenomenon of the trend may be approached. Lao-tzu said, "When 'everyone knows' beauty is beauty, this is ugly; when 'everyone knows' good is good, this is not good."

* * *
* *

Talk and action

> Confucius said, "I used to listen to what people said and trusted they would act on their words. Now I listen to what they say and observe whether they act on their words."

A Zen proverb says, "Don't judge others by yourself." It is obviously wrong to project our own shortcomings on others; it is less obviously, but not less actually, wrong to project our own strengths on others. If you unconsciously attribute to others qualities you expect of yourself, this may lead to unreasonable expectations, resulting in failure and disappointment.

Confucius also added to the above remarks, "It was within my power to do this," meaning that he realized he did not have the power to see to it that people did as they said, he had only the power to see for himself whether or not people did as they said. This attitude is not only less of a burden on all concerned, it is more enlightening because less attention is stolen by emotional conflict.

* * *
* *

Individualism and society

> Confucius said, "Be strict, but not contentious. Associate with others, but do not join factions."

This is a formula for an individualism that is genuinely individualistic without compromising social duty. In this view, to be an individual means to take responsibility for oneself, not to compare oneself with others. Social duty is an acknowledgment of the actual interdependence of all members of society, not the deliberate cooperation of some for their own sake and to the detriment of others.

If it seems extremely difficult to realize these ideals

in their pure form, this would be for the basic reason that in this system of thought ideals are conceived to motivate humanity to progress. By reference to ideals, it is believed, people can accustom themselves to a feeling of humility and a sense of inspiration that cannot for all practical purposes be otherwise acquired.

* * *

Truthfulness and seriousness

Confucius said, "When you stand, see truthfulness and seriousness there before you; when you are in a chariot, see truthfulness and seriousness at the reins. Then you can act effectively."

Without truthfulness, seriousness may be little more than an exaggeration of personality or subjective obsession; without seriousness, truthfulness has no way of expression in the world.

* * *

Promotions

Confucius said, "Promote the honest over the crooked, and people will go along. Promote the crooked over the honest, and people will not obey."

Confucianism has often been portrayed, from both within and without Chinese tradition, as a philosophy of unquestioning obedience to authority and conformity to the status quo.

Original Confucianism, however, as exemplified by the sayings of Confucius himself, was not like this. Confucius taught thinking people to distinguish natural authority based on moral and mental development from man-made authority based on economic, political, technical, and military development.

It was the cherished vision of Confucius to see natural authority and political authority restored to the original unity in which he believed; therefore he regarded the selection of cabinet members and appointed officials to be the greatest responsibility of the rulership.

Being at the top meant that rulers could actually do very little in the way of seeing to it that things were really done as they were supposed to be; so the empowerment of honest and worthy people to operate a chain of authority was a practical necessity.

This is the crux of the problem of all large organizations, which therefore require the inclusion of human development systems either in their own structures or in their milieus in order to operate successfully in terms of their internal functions and external relations.

* * *
* *

Haste and pettiness

Confucius said, "Do not wish for speed, do not pay heed to small advantages. If you wish for speed you will not succeed, and if you pay heed to small advantages you will not accomplish great things."

This may apply to all sorts of activities and endeavors: creating and maintaining a household, raising children, working at a trade or profession, cultivating the intellectual or artistic sensibilities, pursuing an aim in life. Lao-tzu said, "A great vessel takes a long time to complete."

* * *
* *

Making mistakes

Confucius said, "If you make a mistake and do not correct it, that is called a mistake."

The illustrious Zen master Yuanwu said, "Who makes no mistakes? This is why self-correction is what is valued." Since the mistake is in not correcting a mistake, avoidance mechanisms like self-justification, rationalization, or blaming others turn into worse mistakes than the original mistake. Lao-tzu said, "It is by knowing the sickness of sickness that sages avoid being sick."

* * *
* *

Self-correction

> Confucius said, "If you can correct yourself, what problem would leadership be for you? If you cannot correct yourself, however, what can you do about correcting others?"

Confucius believed, with considerable evidence to back him up, that people tended to disrespect and disobey rulers and officials who did not themselves honor the laws and norms they represented.

On another level, this means that without facing up to your own shortcomings and faults and working out compensation and amendment, you cannot develop the insight into human nature required to be a leader or advisor of others.

* * *
* *

Worry

> Confucius said, "Ignoble people are not for positions of authority, because they worry about getting something; and once they have gotten whatever it is they want, then they worry about losing it. As long as they are worried about losing something, there is no telling what they might do."

Please pay particular attention to the conclusion of the argument. According to *The Art of War,* even if you want to defeat opponents, you should not put them in a position where they feel so desperate that they lash out in the blind fury of a cornered or dying beast.

* * *
* *

Calmness

> Confucius said, "Be even-tempered and clear-minded, not always fretting."

Zen masters call this a state of unconcern, or "no-thing." They advise people, furthermore, not to "make a thing of no-thing," for "time and again concern is born of unconcern."

In plain language, evenness of temper and clarity of

mind are considered useful states, attained by the practice of calm; but when these states are turned into objects of concern in themselves, this very concern with equanimity and clarity magnifies the influence of disturbance and confusion on the person so concerned.

* * *
* *

A barometer

Confucius said, "People make mistakes according to their individual type. When you observe people's errors, you can tell their human character."

This is a particularly useful lesson for people in positions of management and leadership. The least of the benefits of this practice is the transformation of anger and disappointment into knowledge and understanding.

* * *
* *

Difficulty and ease

Confucius said, "It is better to be easy to work for but hard to please than to be hard to work for but easy to please. To be easy to work for but hard to please means to refuse

> to be pleased arbitrarily, and to consider individual capacities when delegating tasks. To be hard to work for but easy to please means to be susceptible to being pleased by certain things regardless of whether they are right or wrong, and to expect everything of employees regardless of their individual capacities."

To be exacting without being demanding is a condition of authentic leadership, the mastery of appropriate employment; in everyday terms, choose the right person for the job and it will be done without force or pressure.

To be demanding without being exacting is a symptom of personal intoxication with the power of command; since the attention is mostly on subjective satisfactions, perception of objective realities is unreliable and ineffective.

* * *
* *

Serenity and aloofness

> Confucius said, "It is better to be serene without aloofness than to be aloof without serenity."

To be serene without aloofness means to be actively involved in the world without being trapped by mundane aggravations; to be aloof without serenity means to aggravate oneself by trying to avoid mundane things.

* * *
* *

People and words

> Confucius said, "You lose people if you do not talk to those worth talking to; you lose words if you talk to those not worth talking to. The intelligent do not lose people and do not lose words."

It is an interesting exercise to examine oneself in terms of whether one is losing people or losing words. Usually we lose both at one time or another. Something for each individual to note is which kind of loss demands most immediate remedial work. If you find that you tend to lose people, you may need to cultivate the habit of reaching out to what is best in others. If you find that you tend to lose words, you may need to cultivate the habit of silencing impulsiveness in yourself.

* * *
* *

Good and bad

> Confucius said, "The best people foster the
> good in others, not the bad. The worst peo-
> ple foster the bad in others, not the good."

Master this statement and you can dispense with a
thousand books on leadership and management.

* * *

Humanness

> Confucius said, "You are worthy of the
> name *human* if you can practice five things
> in this world: respectfulness, magnanimity,
> truthfulness, acuity, and generosity."

Confucius regarded humanity, or humaneness, as
the cardinal virtue to be practiced in this life, but he
found so much depth therein that it was very difficult for
him to define his idea of humaneness in all of its parti-
culars. Thus there are many passages in his sayings dealing with this subject but none that go further than this
one in specifying those items that distinguish a human
from a beast.

* * *

Justice

Confucius said, "Avoid both rejection and attachment, and treat people with justice."

Rejection and attachment refer to subjective prejudices, which obstruct the capacity for impartial observation and evaluation. According to a Zen saying, "They are wise who can see what is good about what they dislike and can see what is bad about what they like." But for this impartiality, there is no practical way to treat people justly and without prejudice.

* * *
* *

Study and thought

Confucius said, "Study without thought is blind, thought without study is dangerous."

Without thought, study is not absorbed; without study, thought is uninformed.

* * *
* *

Incompetent leadership

Confucius said, "If you punish people without having admonished them, this is

cruel. If you test them without having in-
structed them, this is brutal. If you are lax
in direction and yet make deadlines, this is
vicious. If you are stingy in giving what is
due to others, this is being bureaucratic."

These remarks are essential reading for people in positions of leadership and command. It is noteworthy that
Japanese management of foreign-based branch facilities is
often criticized for behavior toward workers contrary to
the principles set out here by Confucius. On close examination, this lapse would seem to be due more to Japanese
discomfort and reticence in foreign cultural and linguistic
milieus than to lack of familiarity with the classical Confucian ideals.

* * *
* *

Seriousness, loyalty, and enthusiasm

Confucius said, "Be dignified, and people
will be serious. Be sociable and kind, and
people will be loyal. Promote the good, in-
struct the unskilled, and people will be en-
thusiastic."

This is a formula for leadership at all levels. Like other such formulas, it is an echo of the central Confucian idea that declarations and regulations are not enough to govern, that leadership needs to embody in itself the conduct it seeks of its people.

* * *
* *

Deference, generosity, and justice

> Confucius said, "Be deferential in your own conduct, be respectful in the service of employers, be generous in taking care of people, and be just when employing others."

The communists rejected Confucianism as an ideology of the upper classes. The masses should have been so lucky as to have been ruled by people who really believed in principles of Confucius such as we have here. Confucius directed many of his remarks at the ruling classes because their power made it so urgent that they become civilized and conscientious rather than self-indulgent and rapacious. There are also many remarks, furthermore, that are aimed at helping people do their best in whatever station or walk of life they may be; and this breadth of concern and compassion was indeed one of the marks of leadership in Confucius himself.

* * *
* *

Home, work, and society

Confucius said, "Be respectful at home, serious at work, and faithful in human relations."

Any questions?

* * *
* *

Justice and profit

Confucius said, "Superior people understand justice, small people understand profit."

Earlier Chinese classical literature speaks of just profit, or the harmonization of justice and profit: "Justice is the root of profit." By the time of Confucius the alienation of justice and profit had reached the stage illustrated by this statement. The ancient idea was later restored (and expanded) in Chinese Buddhist terminology when the characters for *justice* and *profit* were put together to mean "proper benefit," in reference to the beneficial effects of appropriate practices or actions.

* * *
* *

RESOURCES

The Essential Confucius, translated and presented by Thomas Cleary (San Francisco: Harper San Francisco, 1992).

A new collection of the sayings of Confucius, arranged by topics according to his aphorisms on the *I Ching.*

I Ching: The Tao of Organization, translated by Thomas Cleary (Boston: Shambhala Publications, 1988).

A basic textbook of neo-Confucianism by Cheng Yi, one of the founders and greatest masters of the neo-Confucian movement.

Worldly Wisdom: Confucian Teachings of the Ming Dynasty, translated and edited by J. C. Cleary (Boston: Shambhala Publications, 1991).

A collection of sayings of later neo-Confucian practitioners.

Zen Lessons: The Art of Leadership, translated by Thomas Cleary (Boston: Shambhala Publications, 1988).

A classical compendium of what might be called Zen Confucianism, writings on parallel social and spiritual development.

Taoism

* * *
* *

Desire and observation

> Lao-tzu said, "Whenever you are dispassionate, you can thereby observe what is subtle. Whenever you have desires, you can thereby observe what you seek."

Quasi mystics take detachment for a resting place; Taoists use it as a way to see. Quasi mystics regard desire as something to avoid; Taoists use it as a way to see. Both ways of seeing are necessary parts of the operation of the complete mind. It is not possible to attain objective understanding without understanding subjectivity; and it is not possible to evaluate subjectivity truthfully without objective understanding.

* * *
* *

Blinders of convention

> Lao-tzu said, "When 'everyone knows' that 'good' is 'good,' this is not good."

This is not good because in practice "everyone knows" actually means "everyone thinks." When there is no room for another view and society's mind is closed on a given subject, it has excluded itself from any further understanding or capacity to deal rapidly and effectively with changes and new realities. This is in fact what often happened in China when official ideology was backed by massive institutional enforcement; and this is why Taoism often had to work outside conventional channels or else invent new modes of expression as yet unshackled by "everybody knows" conservatism.

* * *
* *

Continuing success

> Lao-tzu said, "All beings work. If they are not possessive or presumptuous in the way they live and act, and they do not dwell on their own successes, then this will ensure continuing success."

Squandering the fruits of success is one way of failure. Personal wealth is squandered by greed; social wealth is squandered by arrogance.

* * *
* *

Blowhards

> Lao-tzu said, "Big talkers reach the end of their wits over and over again. It is better to remain centered."

We all know people whose mouths seem to work faster than their minds. Lao-tzu also says that trust is lost by placing too much faith in words. Other aspects of effective action may be lost as well if talk itself becomes the center of attraction.

* * *

Survival and fulfillment

Lao-tzu said, "Sages go first by putting themselves last, survive by disregarding themselves. It is by their selflessness that they manage to fulfill themselves."

Lao-tzu's formula for being invulnerable is to avoid contention: "Just because I contend with no one, no one can contend with me." Far from being passive and ineffective, as aggressive people are often inclined to believe of it, this Taoist noncontention is a tremendously powerful and efficient manner of dealing with the world. As Lao-tzu also says, the flexible are strong, the stiff snap.

* * *

Forms of goodness

Lao-tzu said, "Goodness in words means being trustworthy. Goodness in government means being orderly. Goodness in work means being capable. Goodness in action means being timely. Yet extremes are avoided only by not being contentious."

Among the most popular clichés about so-called philosophical Taoism is that it rejects Confucian morality and preaches habitual disengagement or withdrawal from the affairs of the world. Lao-tzu's sayings on goodness are enough to dismiss this debilitating misconception, which has taken in many Western scholars since the nineteenth century. The characteristic Taoist stamp on the ideas expressed here is in the last statement about avoiding extremes by not being contentious; this is what maintains the goodness of goodness and preserves it from spoilage.

* * *
* *

Moderation

Lao-tzu said, "It is better to stop then to keep on filling."

This is because to keep on filling leads to overflow, waste, and sorrow. If you haven't observed this already, read some history. It hardly matters what nation or epoch you choose, because the principle is illustrated time and again throughout the human story. For some extra poignancy, however, you might want to read up on the intro-duction and aftermath of a war of your choice. Often it seems that the question is not one of whether this principle of stopping in time applies but a matter of whether it is realized in time.

* * *

Accumulating debts

> Lao-tzu said, "When the rich upper classes are haughty, their legacy indicts them."

So if you want to understand today's problems, read in them the indictments of former generations. Lao-tzu suggests that we do more than this, however, and go on to remove the arrogance and extremes from our personality inheritance so that the exaggerated pressures of the situations they create may be taken from the backs of our heirs.

* * *

Understanding and innocence

> Lao-tzu said, "Can you remain innocent even as understanding reaches everywhere?"

It is essential to encompass both aspects of this saying, innocence and understanding. Innocence that is equivalent to ignorance or naïveté may be an insecure and perilous condition, dependent upon psychological insulation. The real challenge is to be innocent and unaffected in spite of whatever may confront you. Only thus, in fact, can knowledge be safely extended beyond the boundaries of convention.

It may be difficult, for example, to observe human shortcomings and failures without becoming cynical to a degree; it is only by innocence, inward awareness of the sublime origin and latent potential of humanity, that it is possible to understand human weaknesses intimately without losing the constructive indomitability without which such understanding has no practical meaning except ingratitude and despair.

* * *
* *

Balance

Lao-tzu said, "Both favor and disgrace are upsetting."

Those who are favored are prone to worry that the favor may lapse, and also suffer from the envy of the envious; those who are disgraced worry that the disgrace may never be cleared, and also suffer from the gloating of gloaters.

There is no end of examples and illustrations of this principle, and anyone can and should conduct an independent survey of what happens to people when they are favored and disgraced.

A successful career may be as hard on the body and mind as an unsuccessful one; then even if the origin of the distress may be different in each case, the effective nature of the stress progressively converges on sameness for all.

A primary reason that alcoholism is generally found in its severest forms in the extreme upper and lower ends of any society may be stated by precisely this observation of Lao-tzu that "both favor and disgrace are upsetting."

The great Japanese Zen master Bunan said that the rich suffer from their riches while the poor suffer from their poverty. This is another reflection of the same principle. Strangely, it would seem that it is no easier for the rich to relieve themselves of their riches than it is for the poor to relieve themselves of their poverty.

If this seems like a conundrum, please remember it and think on it from time to time.

It is for this reason that the ancient Taoists considered a just equilibrium in society to be a matter in the category of health and hygiene, not abstract morality; a matter of natural reason, not philosophical rationale.

* * *
* *

Egotism

> Lao-tzu said, "The reason we have a lot of trouble is that we have selves."

The trouble to which Lao-tzu refers includes everything from the work involved in upkeep of the physical body to the toilsome vexation of trying to assess whatever happens in terms of its benefit or harm to oneself. Curiously, the solution to the problem is not self-denial or self-mortification as usually understood, because these still revolve around self-concern.

What makes this aspect of Taosim seem vague and remote to Westerners is the Judaeo-Christian tendency to moralize issues that Taoists are inclined to view as pragmatic and strategic matters. Step aside for a moment now and then to behold your self in its various inward and outward guises and roles. See this clearly, as though you were observing other people who concealed nothing, and you may very well find that you now know how to know for yourself whether or not you need to do anything about your self.

* * *
* *

Getting the most for your money

Lao-tzu said, "By not wanting fullness, it is possible to use to the full and not have to make anew."

Use it at full blast and it wears out fast: body, mind, matter, machine—all burn in the same furnace. The same can be said for human relationships in themselves: given time, like a fruit-bearing tree growing to natural maturity, a relationship may continue unfolding and renewing its development and satisfaction throughout its lifetime; whereas if pushed, pulled, and squeezed for every possible bit of stimulation and gratification at the maximum possible rate, it does not take an imbecile to tell an idiot what will soon become of it.

* * *
* *

The highest nobility

Lao-tzu said, "Impartiality is the highest nobility."

The nobility of impartiality is concern for objective truth above subjective inclinations. This is a sine qua non of authentic leadership, a quality whose exercise also tends to precipitate reactions by which the real characteristics of subordinates may be known for what they are.

It is not easy to attain impartiality, no matter how attractive the idea may seem. The nobility of impartiality may be so intellectually appealing, for example, as to lead one into the error of equating equality with sameness, or nondiscrimination with being indiscriminate.

One way to begin cultivating objective impartiality without succumbing to false ideas of its nature is by noticing the good in what you dislike and the flaws in what you like, then putting both to one side for the moment and observing what you neither like nor dislike and thus may scarcely ever notice at all.

* * *
* *

Perspective

Lao-tzu said, "Knowing the constant gives an impartial perspective."

When you measure things in relation to feelings and trends, which inevitably fluctuate and change, being in their context you regard these measurements as durable qualities of whatever you happen to be evaluating. When you understand how changing feelings and trends affect your perceptions of things, however, you come to understand them in a larger context. Then you need not be limited by perceptions corresponding to temporary subjective conditions, and yet you can take them duly into account and not have to ignore them in order to avoid being swayed into biased attitudes.

* * *
* *

Mistrust

Lao-tzu said, "When faith is insufficient and there is mistrust, it is because of placing too much value on words."

When people know that noble sentiments can be parroted and are parroted, and that fine words can be sold and are sold, then they know that they have to look elsewhere for assurances of truthfulness. Then again, when people are more worried about how things are said than about what things are said, their basis of judgment is no longer substantial and their ability to believe is no longer reliable.

* * *
* *

Inner work

> Lao-tzu said, "See the basic, embrace the unspoiled, lessen selfishness, diminish desire."

It is extremely important to take these as four steps in a natural sequence. This needs to be stressed even if obvious, because the last item of a series tends to be freshest since it is the one most recently seen or heard; and in this case people see "diminish desire" and start to worry, thus spoiling the whole process.

First see the basic; then you can embrace the unspoiled. When you have embraced the unspoiled, you become less selfish. When you are less selfish, you do not want to consume more than you need.

If you attempt to do this backward, trying to make yourself want less and force yourself not to be so selfish, you will probably find that your sense of the unspoiled and perception of the basic are about as keen as the feeling of scratching an itching foot from the outside of your shoe.

* * *
* *

Economics

> Lao-tzu said, "Economy is gain, excess is confusion."

Use less and there's more left over. When there are too many concerns, furthermore, choices come to be made for the sake of time, and judgment becomes fragmented thereby.

* * *
* *

Society

Lao-tzu said, "Be tactful and you remain whole."

Lao-tzu does not suggest dishonesty or flattery, methods that dishonest flatterers may call tact but fall far short of what Taoist thinkers meant by this term. A favorite reminder of the Taoist principle of tact is Chuang-tzu's saying that expert tiger keepers know not to feed tigers with live animals or even with whole carcasses, "for fear of the fury of the killing and the rending."

* * *
* *

Ideal people

Lao-tzu said, "Ideal people keep on the move by day without leaving their equipment; though they have a look of prosperity, their resting place is transcendent."

Keeping on the move by day means not stagnating in the course of everyday life; and when you do so without leaving your equipment, this means that you do not move or act at random just for the sake of movement and action but always maintain connection with what is of genuine meaning and value.

The ability to preserve this connection with true meaning and value enables the individual to work in the world successfully, but the real source of this success is not a mundane thing. This is why it is not enough to imitate the outwardness of successful people in order to become successful oneself; it is necessary for each individual to personally tap the very source of success.

* * *
* *

Save or waste

Lao-tzu said, "It is good to save people, so that no one is wasted. It is good to save things, so that nothing is wasted."

According to the Huainan masters—early followers of Lao-tzu who briefly acted as political advisors to a local king in ancient China—equality means that everyone and everything can find a place in society where their specific capacities are usefully engaged; it does not mean that everyone is supposedly regarded as exactly the same. Equality and sameness are not the same thing and are not equal in effective meaning.

When there is too little real diversity in the choices existing within a society or an organization, there tends to be a polarization of conformists and misfits who take conformity and nonconformity to counterproductive levels, resulting in a secondary tension that is not creative but destructive.

When people who are different all strive to do the same thing, the result is not equality but merely that virtually everything except currently "in" convention is neglected, the independent free will of the individual turns into a vestigial organ, and society loses its ability to adapt to changing needs rapidly enough to avoid massive human suffering.

* * *
* *

Curing sickness

Lao-tzu said, "Remove extremes, remove extravagance, remove arrogance."

Traditional Taoist methods for removing extremes, extravagance, and arrogance are noncontention, stopping at sufficiency, and objective self-understanding.

* * *
* *

Effectiveness

> Lao-tzu said, "The good are effective, that
> is all; they do not try to grab power thereby.
> They are effective but not conceited, effec-
> tive but not proud, effective but not arro-
> gant. They are effective when they have to
> be, effective but not coercive."

These beautiful lines describe a critical distinction
between efficacy and aggression. The effective can win
many allies by their effectiveness; the ambitious, con-
ceited, proud, and arrogant can create many enemies by
their ambition, conceit, and pride. This is a way of seeing
the difference between real leaders and despots.

On one level of interpretation, this statement also
describes a method of discerning truth and falsehood in
spiritual teachings and teachers; they are supposed to be
effective according to necessity, not to become tyrannical
captors of lost souls.

* * *
* *

Safety

> Lao-tzu said, "By knowing when to stop,
> you are spared from danger."

One of the ways failure tries you is by tempting you to recoup your losses, including loss of face. One of the ways success tries you is by tempting you to forget your limitations and overreach yourself. Whichever way things are breaking for you, by keeping this perspective of knowing when to stop you can avoid the pitfalls of compulsiveness and thus be spared from its dangers.

* * *
* *

Knowledge

Lao-tzu said, "Those who know others are wise, those who know themselves are enlightened."

In *The Art of War,* the master strategist Sun-tzu says that if you know yourself and others, you will never be engangered in battle; if you know yourself but not others, you will win half your battles and lose half; if you do not know yourself or others, you will be in danger in every single battle.

* * *
* *

Power

Lao-tzu said, "Those who overcome others are powerful, those who overcome themselves are strong."

Defining the word *jihād,* meaning "struggle" but usually translated as "holy war" in Western journals, the prophet Muhammad said that the struggle with oppressors is the lesser *jihād,* and the struggle with the cravings of the ego is the greater *jihād.* He is reported to have said, "We return from the lesser struggle to the greater struggle." This principle is of utmost importance for those who attain to success in the world at some time in their lives.

* * *
* *

Wealth

Lao-tzu said, "Those who are contented are rich."

Is it really any wonder when drug addiction is rife at all levels of a society that embraces a culture of craving?

* * *
* *

Government and service

Lao-tzu said, "In governing people and serving God, nothing compares to frugality."

The church of the early Taoists was roofed with the sky and floored with the earth, heated by the sun and cooled by the wind. And according to the sayings of the early Taoists, the best of the ancient governments were so minimal that the people only heard of them.

Later reformations in religion and politics throughout the world can be seen to have begun by trying to restore this principle and to have ended by trying to forget it.

* * *
* *

Change

Lao-tzu said, "The orthodox also becomes unorthodox, the good also becomes ill."

A great deal of time and energy can be lost defending obsolete ways of thinking and acting just because of familiarity and attachment. We may continue to value what was once useful for no other reason than that we have become accustomed to a particular sense of value. One of the most unfortunate perversions of the democratic system is that politicians can exploit sentimental values beyond the point where they have any useful meaning other than this exploitation potential. A truly successful reformer is not one who mollifies popular illusions with spectacular gestures but one who sees the point where right becomes wrong and good becomes ill, making it possible to break the counterproductive force of habit and switch into a progressive and innovative mode.

* * *
* *

Government and public morale

> Lao-tzu said, "People are pure when government is unobtrusive; people are wanting when government is invasive."

Ancient Taoist political theory held that otherwise innocent people would tend to become corrupt when consistently burdened with demands that were extremely difficult for them to fulfill. Confucius also believed that if people were ruled solely by regulations and penalties, they would come to feel no compunction about trying to avoid them, whereas if they were ruled by example, they would obey their leaders without being ordered around.

* * *
* *

Observation

> Lao-tzu said, "Observe yourself by yourself, observe the home by the home, observe the region by the region, observe the nation

by the nation, observe the world by the world."

To observe yourself by yourself is to understand your own capacities and know the extent to which you are fulfilling them; it is not measuring yourself against an arbitrary standard set up by others for yet others.

To observe the home by the home is to understand the workings of a family in terms of the effective interaction of individuals with each other and with the group as a whole; again, not as compared with what other families could be and do with their resources but with what this particular family could be and do with its own resources.

To observe the region, nation, and world by the region, nation, and world follows the model of the family, involving understanding and appreciation of groups on successively larger scales. To observe each grouping in itself means, for example, to see a society or culture in terms of how it meets its own needs and requirements rather than how its individual elements or mechanisms subjectively compare with isolated elements of other societies or cultures.

One of the most useful but more subtle points of this exercise is to understand how evolutionary development can be deliberately induced without need for competition or contention.

* * *
* *

Crimes, calamities, and faults

> Lao-tzu said, "No crime is greater than approving of greed, no calamity is greater than being discontent, no fault is greater than being possessive."

Approving of greed is worse than greed itself, because it nullifies the innate sense of unworthiness mature people feel toward greed. Since greed is an exaggeration of desire, which occurs as a natural impulse in all living beings, anyone might be susceptible to greedy thoughts. It is only the recognition of its unworthiness in humanity that prevents greed from turning into rapacity. Discontent breeds when greediness is accepted as a way of life. Possessiveness is an attempt to soothe the discomfort and insecurity of chronic discontent.

For modern Western people born into a mass society, perhaps the most difficult aspect of understanding these Taoist ideas is not the so-called culture gap between East and West; it is simply to give up thinking of these principles as moral sentiments and realize they are just practicalities.

* * *
* *

Trustworthiness

> Lao-tzu said, "The wise keep their faith and do not pressure others."

If you pressure others without keeping your own promises, this will undermine your reputation and make you ineffective as a leader of others.

* * *
* *

Overcoming the adamant and forceful

> Lao-tzu said, "The flexible overcome the adamant, the yielding overcome the forceful."

Rigidity inhibits successful adaptation to changing circumstances; excessive excitement consumes itself and burns itself out.

* * *
* *

Opposite ways

> Lao-tzu said, "The way of heaven is to reduce excess and fill need. The way of men

is otherwise, stripping the needy to serve
the excessive."

This passage is an illustration of Taoist ideas of good
and bad government and taxation.

* * *
* *

Stiffness and flexibility

Lao-tzu said, "Stiffness is an associate of
death, flexibility an associate of life."

If you fail to adapt to changes in the current of
trends and events, the consequences can be catastrophic.
This is true whether you are concerned with ultimate reality, social reality, or material reality.

* * *
* *

Self-treatment

Lao-tzu said, "The wise know themselves
but do not see themselves; they take care of
themselves but do not exalt themselves."

In this sense, to know oneself means to understand
oneself objectively; not to see oneself means not to regard
oneself as the center of attention. To take care of oneself

means to attend to the requirements of existence; not to exalt oneself means not to consider this maintenance of oneself an end in itself. One might add, from Zen teaching, that the wise use themselves and are not used by themselves.

* * *
* *

The sickness of presumption

Lao-tzu said, "To presume to know what you do not know is sick. It is possible to avoid sickness only by recognizing the sickness of sickness."

In modern times, criticism has so often degenerated into an instrument of destruction that sight is lost of the constructive aim of authentic criticism. Eventually criticism becomes almost an end in itself, with its other main function being to elevate the opinions of critics to the status of objective facts in the minds of the consuming public.

* * *
* *

Underestimating opponents

Lao-tzu said, "No disaster is worse than to underestimate your opponents."

Never believe that what you consider a stupid or unworthy idea cannot dominate the minds of large numbers of people, or that far-reaching power cannot come into the hands of someone you consider a stupid or unworthy person.

* * *
* *

Victory

Lao-tzu said, "When opposing armies clash, the compassionate are the ones who win."

To get the most out of this statement, think about what it means to win. Think about what it means to win in general, and what it means in each instance where the question of winning or losing arises.

* * *
* *

The easy way

Lao-tzu said, "The most difficult things must be done while they are easy; the greatest things must be done while they are small."

Those who are too big for small things eventually find themselves too small for big things. Those who want to achieve dramatic successes may thereby fail to accomplish what is inconspicuous but necessary.

* * *
* *

Shallowness

Lao-tzu said, "If you agree too easily, you will be little trusted."

Try to please everyone and you wind up pleasing no one. Try to be all things to all people and you wind up able to be nothing to anyone. Treasures are hidden because of their value.

* * *
* *

RESOURCES

Back to Beginnings, by Huanchu Daoren, translated by Thomas Cleary (Boston: Shambhala Publications, 1990).
Accessible reflections for lay people, recombining the essences of pristine Taoism and Confucianism.

The Book of Leadership and Strategy, translated and edited by Thomas Cleary (Boston: Shambhala Publications, 1992).
Selections from *Huainan-tzu,* one of the most comprehensive works of early Taoism, connecting the development of the individual with that of the family, state, and world.

The Essential Tao, translated and presented by Thomas Cleary (San Francisco: Harper San Francisco, 1992).
Taoist translations of *Tao Te Ching* and the essential *Chuang-tzu,* two primary texts of Taoism, covering the basic range of classical concepts and practices.

Vitality, Energy, Spirit: A Taoist Sourcebook, translated and edited by Thomas Cleary (Boston: Shambhala Publications, 1991).
An extensive collection of Taoist materials covering a wide spectrum of developments from the original tradition up to modern times.

Wen-tzu, translated by Thomas Cleary (Boston: Shambhala Publications, 1992).
Attributed to Lao-tzu, reputed author of the *Tao Te Ching,* this is one of the last of the classics of the old Taoist tradition, elucidating the principles and practices found in its predecessors.

The Book of Change

* * *

Don't deploy a concealed dragon.

In other words, don't deploy a power when it should be hidden. A power should be hidden as long as it is itself immature and insufficient to affect a situation constructively. A power should also be hidden when the time and circumstances are not meet for positive action.

Then again, there is a power that cannot be deliberately used, and yet it is power; therefore it is called a concealed dragon, lying coiled at the root of things.

If power is used too soon, or if there is a deliberate attempt to employ power that can only emerge spontaneously without selfish will, in either case the power is vitiated and may even wane away altogether.

* * *
* *

Go back before you have gone too far, and you will have good luck.

When you stray from your path or your purpose, the sooner you wake up to the fact and return to your course, the easier it will become to be successful in your endeavors.

Because errant action derives from errant thought, it is most critical to observe your mental state as the basis of your activities. Then it is much easier to "go back before you have gone too far." A Zen proverb says, "When thinking is sick, stopping is medicine."

* * *
* *

It is good to be sensitive, as long as you are sensitive in the right way; you will be lucky if your intentions and your actions are up-right.

Sensitivity can mean vulnerability. Then it is important to be carefully aware of the nature and quality of the influences to which you expose yourself or allow yourself to be exposed.

Sensitivity also means the ability to put your energy at the disposal of a source of stimulus or motivation. Here again it is imperative to consider the inward and outward character of the forces to which you make yourself available.

It is the reality of your intention that attunes you to specific influences or forces that affect your action. The test of uprightness, or correctness, is in the objective effect, not the subjective definition.

* * *
* *

When you are successful, be modest and do not make an ostentatious display of your achievement. While you are pursuing your aim, furthermore, you should avoid attachment to the means you employ in hopes of attaining the desired end. You should be aware, however, that modesty and detachment will be criticized by petty people.

There is a Zen saying that goes, "The spoils of war are ruined by celebration," meaning that self-congratulation and complacency can easily turn into the dark lining inside a silver cloud.

Addictive behaviors and wild mood swings are specialized manifestations of susceptibility to external influences, being heightened by elation through immodest indulgence in what is sensed as a pleasant experience, followed by depression through the removal of the stimulus or the vitiation of its effect.

* * *
* *

You are alarmed when there is a stir, but the effect is good if you use that as a stimulus to bring about improvement.

Because things cannot remain the same forever and must eventually change, it is important to understand the implications of how we react to change. When our sense of security is based entirely on the status quo, on a particular state of affairs external to ourselves, then we can hardly avoid upset when changes take place. Understanding this reaction, we have the option to develop a relationship with the world at large that is more flexible and adaptive, and an inner trust in the power and resourcefulness of the will to live.

Rather than blunt ourselves by trying to control our sensitivity to shock in itself, we can develop sensitivity even further to enhance the educational or inspirational value of slight changes. In this way the evolution of human character and institutions can proceed more smoothly and consciously, without building up unbearable tensions through denial and neglect to a degree where they are liable to burst out so violently as to compromise the future value of the inevitable reaction and adjustment.

Whatever you do, in whatever work you strive, there will always be times when you do not attain your will. This may disturb you, but it will not cripple you as long as you use that disturbance in its proper place as a catalyst for self-understanding and adaptive reaction.

In any relationship, for example, there may be upsets and changes along the way. As in the case of a fevered body, this does not simply mean there is a flaw or malfunction in the system; it also means the system is working to adapt to crises.

* * *
* *

Be upright and true, steady and in control.

When you start out on a basis of strength, the orientation of strength is all-important. It is best to master yourself and not to be impulsive in the use of strength.

* * *
* *

It is bad luck to ignore what you already have and look for something else.

A Zen proverb says, "Gazing at the moon in the sky, you lose the pearl in your hands." People may overlook their own strengths and capacities at the stage where these endowments are still subtle and as yet undeveloped. Yet it is precisely this stage of dormancy that should be examined if the full potential of the individual is ever to be brought into play. Unless there is an awakening from within, nothing added from outside can complete a human being, as emphasized in the oft-forgotten second half of the famous biblical saying, "You are the salt of the earth: if the salt loses its flavor, what can salt it?"

* * *
* *

It bodes well to work together for progress.

Collective effort is especially important when individual power is at a low level. Inwardly, working together means using your own inner resources in a concentrated and directed way; outwardly, it means people cooperating to carry out an undertaking or achieve an aim. When both inward and outward cooperation and coordination are achieved, maximum performance can be realized on both individual and group levels at the same time, in the same endeavor.

* * *
* *

It bodes well to be constant in dedication.

Except for unusual cases of grace or inspiration, in most of human life nothing of importance can be achieved without steady application to its accomplishment. When people work faithfully and consistently at a worthy aim over a long period of time, seldom do they fail to attain success; and the entire process also affects the development of human character itself.

* * *
* *

You can avoid error if you know when to refrain from action.

Progress and success are not just matters of doing the right thing at the right time. It is not only important to act when it is necessary to do so; it is also important not to act when action is useless or counterindicated. In particular, it is best not to use what strengths you have compulsively as long as they are still immature or unfocused.

* * *
* *

When people less capable than you are in need, it is not blameworthy to drop what you happen to be doing in order to help them out; but it is imperative to determine proper measure and avoid excess.

Whatever you are doing may seem to be the most important thing to you at the moment, but in a larger context there may be a greater need for you to help others who are not in a position to help themselves. Since people at home and in society are interdependent upon one another, it is important to consider the balance of self-help and helping others; it is necessary to take care of one's own responsibilities, and it is also essential to do what one can to look after the interests of others. If the one is taken too far, it becomes selfishness and solipsism; if the other is taken too far, it becomes meddling and interference.

* * *
* *

When two people have similar qualities but are not developed to the same degree, if they work together as equals it is possible to raise the level of the less-developed partner.

A Zen proverb says, "When water is level, it does not flow." If you see people only in terms of their similarity, you cannot fully appreciate their differences and learn from them; but if you see people only as different, you cannot make full use of the feelings of sympathy and communality that draw people together and make the interaction of their different qualities a constructive force in their mutual evolution.

* * *
* *

If you want to achieve your end without error, be careful of how you begin.

Lao-tzu says, "The journey of ten thousand miles begins at the first step." It is not only a matter of having the energy and determination to take a step; it is also crucial to consider the questions of how, when, and where to take that step.

* * *
* *

Work on yourself first; take responsibility
for your own progress.

At the outset of an undertaking, when there is potential but no momentum, it may be that all you can do at
first is to marshal your own resources and try to develop
the capacities and qualities you will need along the way.
Without a developed framework of support at this stage,
you will need to manage yourself and do your own work,
under your own steam. If you rely on others before you
have consolidated your own strength and awakened your
own faculties, you may tend to become dependent and
weak.

* * *
* *

As standards change, it is imperative to
choose wisely. You can be effective at this if
you communicate with other people.

Standards of conduct and procedure are originally
adopted, then adapted, to answer the needs of specific
times and circumstances. Eventually they become cus-
tomary; then they are taken for granted. Finally they are
turned into objects of proprietary interest. At that point,
the process of adaptation to change is blocked by con-
servative sentiments, which cling to the forms of estab-

lished standards but forget their original meaning and purpose.

As society and environmental conditions nevertheless change, therefore, as they inevitably do, standards must also change. Thus it is important to exercise good judgment in adopting new standards to suit new situations. The most efficient way to accomplish this is through understanding the special needs of the group or the community in the process of evolving new ways of life.

* * *

If trouble is stopped at once, there is nothing wrong.

It is unrealistic to imagine that anything will go exactly as you wish or that you will encounter no problems in your activities and undertakings. It may often happen that too much time is spent looking for someone to blame when things unexpectedly go wrong. The important thing in such a case is to stop the problem itself as soon as possible. When it is stopped at once, a problem is no longer a problem; but if the reaction is more emotional than practical, continued recriminations will only make more trouble.

* * *

It may be beneficial to undertake a great work, but you will only avoid blame if it turns out very well.

When you have personal power and capacity but lack rank or authority, you may want to do something that is commensurate with your own ability but for which you have no outside support, encouragement, or authorization. In such a case you may well attempt something great, but you should be aware that in the absence of organized backing you will be criticized unless you are unusually successful.

* * *
* *

It is unlucky to act on power impetuously.

The greater your personal power, the greater your need and responsibility to yourself and others to keep your self-control and enhance the inner qualities that give meaning and direction to power.

* * *
* *

When the time is not yet ripe to act, and you are waiting on the fringes of a situation, you will not go wrong if you remain steady and avoid giving in to impulse.

Timing is an essential ingredient of success, and the successful person is one who knows how to wait for the right time before acting. If your acts are impelled by involvement in a situation you are not ready to handle, or by inward impulses you cannot control, then it will be easy to go wrong.

* * *
* *

When there is danger, it is best to desist.

Success depends on acting at the right time and desisting at the right time. When it becomes apparent early on that a course of action will lead into danger, it is better to desist at once than to proceed with vague hopes for the best.

* * *
* *

Enjoyment in harmony with others is auspicious.

If you are enjoying yourself while others around you are in distress, or if you delight in what displeases others, your enjoyment is not likely to continue long. Enjoyment in harmony with others means that there is no selfishness, no envy, and no resentment to mar your happiness. Confucius said, "What you do not like yourself, do not pass on to others."

* * *
* *

You should not mull over the past. If you feel you have lost yourself, still you should not pursue a false image: then you can recover spontaneously. Seeing evil people, be blameless yourself.

Regret over the past is useless unless it is transformed into knowledge for the future. If you find you have strayed from your real nature or lost your true aim, do not let anxiety impel you to seek at random for something to fill that void. Pursuing a false image will only lead you further astray.

* * *
* *

It is good to be prepared. Distractions will make you uneasy.

In any undertaking, intention and effort need to be grounded on a solid foundation before they can be sustained with effect. The groundwork or preparation of intention is self-examination and self-understanding. What are the underlying motives, what are the immediate and final goals? Knowing what you are doing and why you are doing it also forms part of the groundwork of effort, preparing to carry out an undertaking by marshaling and coordinating the necessary psychological, physical, and environmental conditions for success.

This calls for concentration and direct focus on the purpose and process of your endeavor. During this time, concern with extraneous matters saps your energy and causes you to deviate from your purpose. This results in a state of internal discomfort caused by the disparity between your intention and your attention.

*　*　*
*　*

Be centered and harmonious.

Being centered means not leaning toward extremes, not becoming unbalanced by an overwhelming predominance of one quality over others. In this way it is possible to achieve inward harmony within the self as well as outward harmony with the world at large. Inward harmony means your own faculties are working together; outward harmony means people are working together. Both of these are essential ingredients of success.

*　*　*
*　*

When you are mixed up, be careful, and you can avoid fault.

Sometimes situations are too confused to admit of any positive progress at a given time; under these circumstances, the most that can be hoped for is to avoid error. It is best to recognize such conditions for what they are and to concentrate the attention on preventing mishaps rather than attempt to forge blindly ahead.

* * *
* *

There is no regret when you guard the home.

The home is the basis, both metaphorically and literally. External conditions may be unpredictable and unreliable, so guard the home, keeping your inner resources intact, and you have nothing to regret even when things do not go your way.

Even in the midst of a chaotic society, a stable home can safeguard the sanity and well-being of the people of the family. Similarly, self-mastery can safeguard the integrity and viability of the individual even in the midst of uncertain conditions.

* * *
* *

You will be lucky if you proceed without error.

Luck is not something that the successful wait for passively. The successful person is one who beckons luck by meaningful, well-directed effort. When undertakings accurately reflect the needs and demands of the time and circumstances, good luck is nothing mysterious but simply a manifestation of the natural order of things.

* * *
* *

Impulsive actions resulting in failure are faulty.

Successful endeavors are the result of strategic planning, adequate preparation, and appropriate timing. An arrow that is loosed before the bow is fully drawn will not likely reach the target; an arrow that is loosed before the aim is made certain will surely fly wide of the mark. When things go wrong, it is easy to blame other people or external conditions; but when failure is due to one's own impulsiveness, the responsibility belongs to oneself alone.

* * *
* *

You will be faultless if you avoid association with what is harmful. You will be blameless if you realize the danger and struggle against it.

It is naive to underestimate the influence of the outside world on our character and way of life. Becoming impeccable is not simply a matter of inward cultivation; it also calls for good judgment in respect to the environment within which one chooses to live and work. It is important to be alert and learn to recognize what is harmful in order to be able to take intelligent and effective steps to avoid contact with it if possible or to counteract its negative influences in cases where it cannot be completely avoided.

* * *
* *

You will be lucky if you use the appropriate means to return to normalcy, for what blame can there be then?

Sometimes intensity of concentration and effort can lead to an exaggeration or warp in the way you look at things in the course of everyday affairs. Without an overall perspective, therefore, early intimations of success can actually lead you astray from your purpose in life. It is auspicious if you are able to take note of any one-sidedness developing in your character and take appropriate measures to restore a sense of balance and proportion. Then you can be blameless in attitude and conduct.

* * *
* *

There is no blame when you act plainly.

Much that is awry in our actions comes from artificiality. When excessive emphasis is placed on appearances at the expense of substance, the ability to act directly from our inner selves is diminished. The result of too much concern with superficials is a kind of alienation that makes it difficult to get down to real issues and to deal meaningfully with underlying realities. The advantage of simplicity is in its directness, enabling us to lay hold of essentials and to avoid being confused by extraneous matters.

* * *
* *

You will be blameless if you are impartial toward others.

Many faults and errors derive from subjective biases that prejudice relationships, attitudes, and actions. Likes and dislikes can blind us to what is good in people we dislike as well as to what is bad in people we like. When we cannot deal with people fairly and objectively, we lose contact with the real potential of human interaction and wind up blundering because of our own failure to appreciate the true qualities of the people we encounter in the course of living and working.

* * *
* *

If there is no error at the central core, that is auspicious.

External propriety does not compare to inner up-rightness. An outward facade of correctness that is not supported by truth in the heart will ultimately prove to be of no lasting worth. A Zen proverb says, "Falsehoods are hard to uphold."

* * *
* *

Sensitivity in overseeing is good, beneficial all around.

When overseeing a project, it is essential to be con-sciously aware of all its requirements and to be sensitive to the quality of work in progress. When it involves over-seeing others, it is also important to be sensitive to the individual skills, capacities, and personalities of the work-ers. In this way sensitivity benefits everyone concerned, leading to success in the task at hand.

* * *
* *

You will be blameless if you communicate with sincerity.

Faulty communications result in inefficiency and error. Because of the confusion caused by lack of accurate communication, blame may be assigned arbitrarily, so the real cause of the problem may go undetected. If you communicate sincerely, you can clarify the situation at the outset, thereby avoiding fault and blame in the end.

* * *
* *

Balance is correct and brings good fortune.

Extremist tendencies are not found only in political arenas; they generally beckon disaster in any field of endeavor. By maintaining balance and avoiding exaggeration, it is possible to mitigate the effect of negative influences and to avoid backlash against progressive action.

* * *
* *

Only small gains can be made in a dangerous position.

Even if you have knowledge and capacity, environmental circumstances, whether human or natural, may limit your practical ability to achieve your goals. Under such conditions, it is better to content yourself with small gains for the time being rather than imperil future possibilities by rash or impetuous undertakings at an inopportune time.

* * *
* *

Compassion and cooperation lead to future success.

If those who have greater abilities or are more developed do not make common cause with those of lesser ability or lesser maturity, the group or society cannot make progress as a whole. It is by the sympathetic interaction and sharing of people with different qualities and characteristics that collective development can take place with greatest effect.

* * *
* *

Accept others with tolerance, be positive and farsighted in your endeavors, and you can be impartial and balanced in action.

Overall progress in a group, an organization, or a society cannot take place through the actions of an elite acting alone, even if the elite really has superior capacities. It is essential to include the less powerful and less talented so that all can develop through the energy of pooled abilities.

This can only work if solidarity is expressed in understanding and action, in practical undertakings based on a long view. Thus by enlarging the context of understanding what is to be done over time and how it can be accomplished through cooperative effort, inequalities can be transcended and extreme polarization can be avoided.

* * *
* *

It is beneficial to be singleminded and reserved.

For successful achievement of an aim, it is helpful to concentrate your attention and husband your energy. When attention is scattered among various concerns and energy is expended on extraneous matters, it is difficult to develop effective degrees of will power and creative vitality.

* * *
* *

You will be unlucky if you are too withdrawn.

If you are too passive, or if you are too narrow in your preoccupations or ideas, you will miss opportunities. There may be possibilities of which you cannot avail yourself, simply because of limited perspective and unwillingness to reach forward toward new perceptions of untapped potential.

* * *
* *

When action would lead to bad luck, it is beneficial to be firm and abstain, remaining evenminded.

Sometimes excitement or restlessness may lead one into a course of action that reason would indicate inadvisable. It may be that subjective considerations lend compelling appeal to what would appear undesirable to the objective observer. In such cases it is best to be steadfast and not give in to impulse, keeping a level head to avoid unfortunate mistakes.

* * *
* *

When isolated, seek support, and regrets disappear.

As social beings, people cannot be completely effective alone. When you are thwarted by isolation and lack of support, you need to find some way of relating with others usefully. As individual beings, people seek inner security in their souls; this is why they search for truth and also why they sometimes accept assurance instead of truth.

* * *
* *

Hardship ennobles you. It is beneficial to communicate true sincerity. It is unlucky to be aggressive. If you suffer misfortune because of having been aggressive, you have no one to blame but yourself.

It is easy to resent hardship, but if it is faced squarely with calm determination to overcome it, then it can be a positive experience that helps you grow. If you complain and expect others to take responsibility for what you have to do yourself, you are not dealing with the situation in a truly honest manner. If you react to hardships vengefully, you will run into even more trouble. In that case you may blame others, but it is really your own fault.

* * *
* *

When the situation requires gentleness and flexibility, it will not do to be adamant.

A tree that cannot bend in the wind gets broken down or rooted up in a gale. When you are strong, you may unconsciously assume that you can accomplish everything you need to do by means of strength. But there is always a limit to the power of an individual, and there are always situations too delicate to handle with force.

* * *
* *

Unless you develop yourself, you cannot be of much help to others.

Good intentions may turn out to be ineffective if you do not have the means to personally see them through. Compassion impels us to try to help our fellow human beings when we see them in need; wisdom tells us what we can do and what we could do, what we need in ourselves in order to be able to really help others.

* * *
* *

If you are strong, you will do nothing regrettable as long as you are flexible and balanced.

Power or energy of any kind can lull and intoxicate the unwary, leading to indulgence in the experience of power and energy for the sake of the experience itself. This indulgence can result in a blind and aggressive quest for power and exercise of power, without regard for the rights and feelings of others. The greater the power, the greater the need to temper it with harmony and balance.

* * *
* *

Rectitude is auspicious.

When handling power, it is important to avoid becoming so fascinated by it that you begin to feel you can do anything you want without suffering any negative consequences. The more power you command, the more critical the question of how you put it to work. Power without control simply begs the question and creates its own blind momentum. When power is balanced with self-mastery, only then can it be properly directed; power is then the servant and not the master.

* * *
* *

When you are on the brink of a difficult situation, people will talk a little, but if you remain centered and relaxed, it will turn out well in the end.

When problems arise, people who are strong and energetic may address them too hastily because of eagerness to effect speedy resolutions. Immediate action may be contraindicated, however, when to become embroiled in a difficult situation would vitiate strength and energy before anything positive can be effectively accomplished.

When you remain for a time on the periphery of such a situation, awaiting the right time to act, it will appear to others that you are doing nothing; and thus they will be inclined to criticize you for negligence or timidity.

All will be well in the end, however, if you keep your balance, remain calm and objective, and do not let such complaints impel you into acting prematurely.

* * *
* *

Strength should not be used impulsively.

When personal power is in balance, it is stabilized and controlled so that it cannot act out in compulsive behavior. Used flexibly, without adamant aggressiveness, strength is adaptable and responsive, therefore able to harmonize with the needs of the time rather than operate as a self-propelling impulse.

* * *
* *

The joy of truthfulness is auspicious; it makes regret vanish.

To please others merely as a ploy to attain personal ends is to play a dangerous game, making your security depend upon deception. The constant effort to maintain deception diverts creative energy and robs the will of freedom. Conversely, to take pleasure in being the recipient of false flattery undermines the conscience and makes the individual dependent upon an unrealistic idea of the self.

* * *
* *

You can be impeccable if you see the truth
in all situations.

When personal biases and emotional judgments
color perceptions, this can result in an unrealistic response that is out of harmony with real needs and thus
ineffective or even counterproductive. When the first concern is to see truth of a situation, whatever it may be, then
it becomes possible to address problems or needs in a
manner that is accurate and to the point, not distorted by
subjective expectations or wishful thinking.

* * *
* *

Even if you are not given recognition, keep
working sincerely and your heart's desire
will come to you. When you are fulfilled,
you share with others spontaneously.

Do not be discouraged if others do not understand
or acknowledge what you are doing, as long as you are
clear about your own purpose. If you continue to make
an honest effort, you will surely be rewarded for it. Take
care of the cause, and you need not worry about the effect. When you finally succeed in your aim, the results of
your efforts will naturally become part of the experience
of your associates and other people around you.

* * *
* *

An old and enfeebled organization benefits from an infusion of fresh life.

When the inspiration and energy of an enterprise have waned, it may be impossible to regenerate it fully from within. In that case, there is profit in absorbing new inputs, such as fresh ideas and new personnel, in order to revitalize the operation.

* * *
* *

If you are inwardly secure, even if people are jealous, luckily they cannot affect you.

When you are insecure in yourself, you may look to others for direction and support. This may be flattering to them, but it increases your inner weakness by habituating you to dependency. When you are inwardly secure, in contrast, people may be resentful and jealous of your independence, but this cannot influence you. Then it is possible to bring forth your abilities to the full without worrying about being resented and ostracized by those who are envious of your success.

* * *
* *

When you are in a position of subordinate responsibility, it is good to keep up frequent and honest communications.

In a position of subordinate responsibility, on the one hand you are in charge of those under you, while on the other hand you are answerable to those above you. It is therefore imperative to maintain good relationships with both subordinates and superiors in order that the entire organization or operation run smoothly, with all involved doing their part in a continuum of efficiency.

The key to good relationships is regular communication, and the key to communication is sincerity. By frequent communications it is possible to keep up with changes in conditions, and by sincere honesty it is possible to connect effectively with the minds and hearts of associates.

* * *
* *

When you have been thwarted, you will escape calamity if you go back home and live unobtrusively.

It is impossible to win every time, to succeed in all your undertakings, or to have everything your own way. If you are unsuccessful in something and yet adamantly refuse to acknowledge failure or defeat, or if you take on more than you can handle and are unwilling to recognize situations where you cannot prevail, and instead you arrogantly insist on pressing your suit and contending for victory, you may bring disaster on yourself. If you know when you have had enough and accept your limitations honestly and gracefully, resting content with your lot and living within your means, then you can avoid unnecessary trouble and will not be crushed even in defeat.

* * *
* *

It is lucky for people to lead each other back to normalcy.

When some aspect of your life has become exaggerated, this in itself will bias any attempts you may make to restore your own balance. It is therefore important to maintain communicative relationships with other people so that through your association you may help each other to rectify your errors and recover normalcy. You will be particularly fortunate in this respect if you can find people who are wiser and more experienced than you are, for their example and influence can be of inestimable value to you in your own development.

* * *
* *

If the course of action you have taken turns out to be smooth, you will be lucky only if

you are steadfast and inwardly undisturbed
by external things.

Whenever the going is easy, you may become prone
to complacency. This can lead to carelessness, which in
turn makes you susceptible to outside influences. When
you are relaxed and unwary, you may be distracted and
deflected from your course by the appearance of unfore-
seen events. Everyone knows the importance of steadfast-
ness and inward fortitude in the midst of difficulty; these
qualities are even more important to remember in times
of ease, for the very fact that they are readily forgotten in
the absence of abrasive conditions. Therefore, when you
are on a smooth course you will ultimately be fortunate
only if you are careful to avoid being deceived by ease,
remaining steady and aloof from outward distractions.

* * *
* *

There is nothing wrong with working on
yourself alone when necessary, but it does
not help those around you just then.

You cannot do for others what you cannot do for
yourself, so it is necessary to develop yourself before you
can be of genuine help to others. To work on your own
development may therefore be in fact altruistic when it
appears to be selfish; but at the stage when you are con-

centrating on self-work, the benefit this may have for others in the future has not yet materialized and is therefore not yet apparent to those around you.

* * *
* *

When in an unsettled state, it is well to practice moderation.

If you exercise strength immoderately while in an unsettled condition, you are likely to lose balance and go too far. Even if you have the energy to act, if the situation is uncertain you may misapply your efforts and thereby increase confusion. Therefore it is best to control yourself under such conditions and to avoid acting impulsively.

* * *
* *

When inner power begins to manifest outwardly, it is beneficial to be exposed to enlightened guidance.

Power without meaningful direction is worse than weakness, inasmuch as it poses the danger of arbitrary and uncontrolled exercise of force. When energy is built up within you and begins to appear in your outer life, it is especially important to look to worthy exemplars to guide you in its useful employment.

* * *
* *

Humble workers who accomplish their
end will be lucky.

Humility is a useful quality insofar as it reduces fric-
tion. It smooths the path of human relationships and enables you to derive maximum benefit from association
with others, freeing you from the baggage of egotistical
contentiousness. Humility also allows you to pursue a
goal patiently, without being inhibited by making unrealistic demands on yourself.

Elevated to the status of a virtue of value in itself,
humility turns into its opposite and becomes a vice. Taking pride in humility cancels its beneficial effects. Therefore effective humility is not that contrived modesty in
which one secretly takes pride but is, rather, transcen-
dence of the ego whereby environmental resistance is
minimized and undertakings are facilitated. Thus true
humility is known by effect, not by appearance.

* * *
* *

When it is nearly time to emerge from
concealment, do not attempt to effect a
hasty correction of affairs.

When reason and justice are suppressed by the brutality of tyrants (be they human, conceptual, or material tyrants), and conditions are such that there is no present possibility of bringing about improvement by overt action, it may be prudent or even necessary to go into hiding.

To go into hiding may mean removing oneself from the thick of things, or it may simply mean keeping one's ideas to oneself. Depending on conditions, it may also mean intelligent dissimulation. In any event, nothing can last forever, including the oppressive power of tyranny; eventually a time must come when the tide turns and there is potential for positive action.

Eagerness for change, however, added to the force of suppressed feelings, may provoke hasty action before the time is quite right. According to a Zen saying, "What has been long neglected cannot be restored immediately; ills that have been accumulating for a long time cannot be cleared away immediately."

* * *
* *

If there is no resistance, there is no questioning.

When everything seems to be going your way, you may become complacent and act arbitrarily without feeling any need to question your motives and actions. According to a Zen saying, "Calamity can produce fortune" if one becomes earnest and sincere when faced with difficulties, and "fortune can produce calamity" if one becomes complacent and presumptuous when everything is going smoothly. Thus it is said that "sages have worries all their lives and thus never any trouble."

* * *
* *

When you are in the ascendancy, you will be attacked if you do not take precautions; that is unfortunate.

An everyday Japanese proverb says, "The nail that stands out gets hit." This is often used to illustrate the attitude and mechanism of conformism in Japanese society, but it can also be used more generally to illustrate the workings of envy and jealousy. Whenever anyone succeeds at something, or rises to a position of eminence, unfortunately there always seem to be those who attack the successful and strive to encompass their downfall. Understanding this aspect of human psychology, the prudent will be wary of attracting the envy of others. It was for this very reason that ancient Zen masters spoke of eschewing fame and embracing humility.

* * *
* *

Turn back on seeing danger.

Ancient Taoist philosophy places great value on knowing when to stop. If you see that a course of action will lead to perilous situations, it is much better to stop and turn back than to proceed blindly ahead hoping for the best. To be safe, therefore, it is important to be able to foresee danger while it is still possible to avert it. This is one of the primary functions of *The Book of Change* itself—honing insight into the nature of events as the working out of predictable processes.

* * *
* *

Inflexibility is fatal, too much ambition is dangerous.

If you cannot adapt to changes, you eventually lose contact with the realities of the times. If you are unable to put yourself in others' positions you cannot understand them or communicate with them effectively. Thus inflexibility puts you at a disadvantage in both professional and social life.

This is especially true when you are inflexible in the sense of being adamant about your personal ambitions, insisting on achieving predetermined goals regardless of anything or anyone else. In such a case your ambitions will imperil you because you have no way to avoid head-on confrontations with people or situations that seem to stand in your way.

* * *
* *

You cannot be comfortable forever; when hard times come, be steadfast.

Everything is in a state of flux; the fact of life that does not change is change itself. In an unpleasant state of affairs this realization can bring joy; in a pleasant situation this awareness can bring sorrow. It is particularly important to remember the reality of change when things are going well, in order to head off the consequences of the complacency, arrogance, and presumption that can readily develop under such conditions.

There is an ancient maxim of martial artists and strategists that applies just as well to other fields of endeavor: "When you have won, behave as if you had not." When you are successful, if you remember that change comes like the wind and thus consciously avoid falling into routine expectations, then you can be steadfast when hardship and difficulty arise. In this way you will be able to survive well under any circumstances.

* * *
* *

It is counterproductive to employ too much strength.

Everything has its proper measure, anything short of which will not do the job and anything beyond which may spoil the result. To use force in a situation that calls for tact ruins harmony; to use strength instead of skill brings on many blunders. The fundamental teaching of *The Book of Change* hinges on the need to temper strength with yielding, moderating firmness with flexibility to achieve an effective balance of complementary qualities.

* * *
* *

Use the best of yourself to overcome negative influences.

When you are beset by frustrating problems, it is important to avoid letting them have a decisive influence on your mood, because the frame of mind thus created will tend to beckon its own kind in the form of further frustrations and problems. You will have a better chance of surviving well under negative conditions, and even of ultimately thriving, if you are able to reach into your inner reserves and draw forth your most positive qualities. If you can discover hidden strength untouched by external influences, by nurturing and fostering that strength you may overcome conditions that would otherwise thwart you and inhibit you from fulfillment.

* * *
* *

It is good to always be upright when successful.

When success leads to complacency, inflation of the ego, and disregard for others' problems and concerns, then it will eventually turn into failure through loss of the qualities necessary to renew and maintain successful undertakings. Therefore rectitude and honesty are all the more necessary when one becomes successful, to avoid being spoiled by the fruits of success.

* * *
* *

As long as you are really alert, there is no worry even if people try to take you unawares.

You cannot necessarily prevent people from behaving in aggressive ways toward you, and you cannot necessarily make yourself invulnerable to attack; but if you are watchful, you can foresee such problems and avoid them by removing yourself from the line of fire before anything serious happens.

* * *
* *

When you have great capacity for bearing responsibility, if you have an aim you will be impeccable.

Someone may have a goal without having the means to achieve it; another may have the power to achieve great things without the direction to guide it. The one who has the goal but lacks the means may become an idle dreamer or an embittered failure; the one who has the power but lacks direction may become a bully or a pawn. Only when you have both the capacity to accomplish works and a worthy aim to guide it can you be impeccable in your actions.

* * *
* *

Immature people exploit power; mature people do not.

Power is one of the severest tests of character. If it goes to your head, you may become an egotistical tyrant. Power employed to aggrandize individual personalities cannot be used effectively for the benefit of society as a whole. Mature people are those able to master themselves and avoid abuse of power.

* * *
* *

RESOURCES

The Buddhist I Ching, by Chih-hsu Ou-i, translated by Thomas Cleary (Boston: Shambhala Publications, 1987).

An analytic interpretation and commentary on the classic from political, social, religious, philosophical, and psychological viewpoints.

I Ching: The Book of Change, translated by Thomas Cleary (Boston: Shambhala Publications, 1992).

A unique translation of the core text of the classic, with essential commentary and explanation traditionally attributed to Confucius himself. In pocket-book format.

I Ching Mandalas, translated by Thomas Cleary (Boston: Shambhala Publications, 1988).

A set of programs for organizing, analyzing, reading, and consulting the classic to yield a highly intensified systems-generating core.

The Taoist I Ching, by Liu I-ming, translated by Thomas Cleary. (Boston: Shambhala Publications, 1986).

An in-depth elucidation of the classic from a pragmatic neo-Taoist point of view. Also includes "The Confucian Changes," a neo-Taoist explanation of key commentaries attributed to Confucius.

Teachings on
the Art of War

* * *

Flexibility

Sun-tzu said, "Structure your forces strategically, according to what will be beneficial or advantageous."

Keep flexibility in the mechanism of organizational structuring and operation so that setups can shift and regroup with maximum efficiency in response to changes or special needs that arise with time.

* * *
* *

Deception

Sun-tzu said, "Warfare involves deception."

In struggle, appear to be as you are not, so that you cannot be pinned down or figured out. Then you deprive opponents of the advantage of knowing what they are facing and what to expect.

Are things as you yourself figure them to be, or do the projections of others enter into the picture? Try to assess what you are projecting as well as what others are projecting.

Does anyone "have your number?" Does anyone *think* they "have your number"? Do you play to that role, that expectation? Do you use that image as a cover, a camouflage? What for? What else could be accomplished in the room left by people who are dealing with an image of you that is only a projection of their expectations?

* * *
* *

Suckers are made

> Sun-tzu said, "Seduce opponents with the prospect of gain, take them by causing confusion."

Here is a general tactic to think about: Make everyone believe there is more to gain by maximum reliance on foreign trade and currency than by maximum self-sufficiency supplemented by foreign trade in essential items lacking in the domestic economy. Compare your ideas of the results and future consequences of the former tactic and the latter policy.

Here are some questions to think about: Do Americans believe it is better to individually pay less for a better foreign product, if by doing so the domestic industry becomes that much less viable? Should the citizens support domestic industry, if it means greater destruction of the environment through backwardness of local standards and technologies?

Considering the fact that there is a price to pay for everything, a minus for every plus, how can issues become confused by isolating one gain or one loss from its total context and magnifying it out of proportion?

* * *
* *

Anger and disarray

Sun-tzu said, "Anger opponents so as to throw them into disarray."

Making opponents "lose their heads" may be an effective way to diffuse the energy of aggressive people who cannot be successfully met head-on. It may be an effective way to encompass the downfall of the arrogant and complacent.

Consider the energy expended in America on Japan-bashing. This is often an empty and ineffective gesture of frustration. If the same energy were funneled into seeking constructive solutions, there would be a more harmonious situation. A lot of impotent emotion is accepted, nevertheless, because it is useful to politicians as a sideshow for their constituents, in lieu of promising answers to America's loss of face as an industrial power.

Japan would probably rather see America blow off steam consoling itself by Japan-bashing than become more truly competitive. If America is busy enough being angry at others for its own plight, that may well prevent the focus and concentration necessary for genuine solutions from ever developing in the American consciousness.

So when Americans indulge in anger at Japan, they should watch out to see if they are not thereby shooting themselves in the foot with this attitude.

To observe the effects anger has on perceptions, try to cultivate the ability to call up an angry mood at will. There is usually something past or present that you can use to annoy yourself if you think about it. Then use the mood of anger as a lens through which to view other things, and see how they look when you feel this way.

Mastering anger does not necessarily mean suppressing your feelings. Mastering anger first involves understanding how it affects you, learning to take this influence into account, and learning to step aside. By seeing it as a guest and not identifying with it as the host, you can learn to leave anger unused even when it occurs or to divert it to positive inspiration, without losing your effectiveness by expending excess energy on trying to control emotion.

* * *
* *

Humility

> Sun-tzu said, "Feign humility toward opponents to make them arrogant."

When Japan is self-assertive, America gets furious. When Japan is meek, America becomes arrogant. If Japan does not seem to want to take up a position of political leadership in the world, as America often complains, it might be for the reason that nonassertion seems to the Japanese to be a better method of getting their own way.

* * *
* *

Fatigue

> Sun-tzu said, "Tire out opponents by running away from them."

Endless discussions and negotiations in which one side appears to give way but little to nothing actually gets done—this has almost been the norm of U.S.-Japan trade talks.

It probably happens all over the place, a lot of the time. When you see some action, try to determine whether the action is taking place to fulfill its overt function or to make it impossible to do anything else with the time and resources involved.

If it is an interaction, try to find out if all parties see it the same way. If one side thinks the overt aim is the real agenda while the other assumes otherwise, the result can be some fairly comical tragedies and tragic comedies. There again, it depends on the vantage point of the observer.

* * *
* *

THIRTY-SIX STRATEGIES

Sneak over the ocean in plain view.

This strategy involves cultivating a facade to the point where it is taken for granted and thus can be used as a cover to accomplish an ulterior purpose.

The contemporary image of Japan as a peaceful, pacifistic country and the image of Japan as a lightweight in international politics are seldom examined for the value they could have to neo-fascists and militarists.

Because of the peaceful, political-lightweight image, it is possible that contrary tendencies in Japanese government and society could be effectively overlooked, or not taken seriously, until they have grown to proportions that are perceptibly difficult to control.

* * *
* *

Besiege one party in order to rescue another.

This is a ploy whereby a group enters into a dispute on one side, ostensibly as a defender of a beleaguered party, but really to extend its own sphere of influence.

If a nation can actually contribute to the resolution

of socioeconomic problems in foreign locales, it can in effect increase its "territory" with impunity.

If Japan became more independent of the United States in global politics and then went to the aid (as the USSR used to do) of small nations feeling put-upon or exploited by U.S. power, it could increase its sphere of influence under the guise of moral probity.

This is exactly what Japan tried to do with its "Greater East Asia Co-Prosperity Sphere" idea, which was in reality nothing more than a front for Japanese imperialism.

Unlikely as a repeat of the same scheme in the same form may seem to be, the assumption of the impossibility of the unlikely is one of the first omens of defeat in the art of war.

* * *
* *

Borrow another's weapon to kill your own enemy.

This means getting someone else to do your fighting for you. When the United States accuses Japan of being a political lightweight, what this often really means is that Japan will not "lend its sword" to the United States in the arena of global politics to the degree that the United States would like, in view of the actual material power of that sword.

The idea of Japan "accepting its share of the defense burden" could be seen by Japan as an attempt to use it as a "borrowed sword" against enemies of the United States. Japan, however, does not want to be drawn into the middle of political struggles perceived as being in the interests of other nations.

A nation whose economy relies heavily on arms production, on the other hand, might be willing to take up the role of the "borrowed sword" if its military technology has advanced to the point where it feels confident of a favorable cost/benefit ratio.

* * *

Confront those who are tired while you yourself are comfortable.

This means that it is advantageous to see to your own security while getting competitors to run themselves ragged.

Compare education and industry in Japan and in the United States, not only from the point of view of what they are accomplishing but also in terms of the relevant moods and attitudes within those concerns themselves as well as in society at large.

Take particular note of the implications inherent in the claim that Japan is securing world leadership in high technology, finance, and management skills.

Confucius said that one should not fret about not being in a position of power but rather worry about how to become actually competent and qualified to handle power usefully. When you are in the position of the weary and others are in the position of ease, it makes no sense to attack; the advice of Confucius is the indicated remedy for this situation.

* * *
* *

Observe others' problems from a safe vantage point.

This means to look on from a distance when competitors become embroiled in their own internal problems, waiting for them to fall into such a state of dilapidation that they turn into easy pickings for raiders and scavengers.

It would be interesting, in light of this strategy, to make a comparison of how much economic influence Japan wields in the United States vis-à-vis how much Japan contributes to the resolution of socioeconomic problems in the United States.

In more general, global terms, how much do nations take advantage of the resources of other nations, how much do nations take advantage of the problems of other nations, and how much do nations contribute to the welfare of other nations?

* * *
* *

Conceal aggressive intentions behind an ingratiating facade.

An example of this is the Japanese cultural front as it exists on the level sponsored by nationalistic Japanese interests on the premise that Westerners will not feel so much antipathy toward Japan if they have more knowledge and appreciation of Japanese culture, and presumably will therefore resent Japanese economic power to a lesser extent.

This doesn't always work that well, because Americans are not necessarily thrilled by traditional Japanese high culture, and because Americans are not schooled to think of other cultures as even equal to their own, much less superior and more worthy of a position of global leadership.

Another example of this is found in the Americans who learn some Japanese on the premise that it will be of advantage to them in dealing with Japan. This does not always work very well either, because the Japanese do not necessarily regard gestures made for motives of personal profit to reflect authentic interest in any part of their culture except the financial; and if they cannot discern an individual's motives, they will take steps to find out, or if they haven't time for this, simply shun that person (in reality, if not appearance) just for good measure.

Yet another example is the counterpart of ultra-nationalist-inspired Japanese studies abroad: the cliché financed by the foreign interest who wishes to appear to be interested in and even sympathetic to Japanese culture while covertly fostering cultural clashes through promotion of less noticeable if no less influential unrealities and biases.

* * *

One tree is felled for the sake of another.

One of the organizational strengths the Japanese are often able to muster is represented by this stratagem, which basically means the willingness, or recognition of the necessity, for an individual to make a personal sacrifice in the interests of the group. Although self-sacrifice is a Christian virtue in theory, post-Renaissance individualism and the vast possibilities of territorial expansion in a seemingly endless New World have made it difficult for Westerners, particularly Americans, to muster this particular strength to the degree attained in much older civilizations. This, however, may be expected to change in the future.

* * *

Make temporary use of a dead body in order to revive a spirit.

An example of this in Japan is the revival of traditional culture as a focus of national pride, in spite of the fact that traditional culture actually has relatively little to do with everyday life in modern Japan, except for some token observances. Ths use of fossilized traditional high culture as a pacifier or a decoy to capture or divert the attention of factions within the organizations of political and economic rivals would be another example of this strategem.

* * *
* *

Steal a beam from another's structure to replace a pillar in your own.

This is a classic description of what we call head-hunting. This is not practiced as much within Japanese society as it is within American society, but it is definitely practiced by the Japanese on an international level. Numerous high-ranking persons from among U.S. trade negotiators and the U.S. federal bank system have been very profitably head-hunted by Japanese concerns involved in foreign trade.

* * *
* *

Let opponents climb up onto the roof,
then take the ladder out from under them.

An example of this would be Japan and other countries taking over the manufacturing sector while the United States turns to the service sector. If service and management are viewed as resting on a foundation and support structure of primary and secondary production (agriculture and industry), the metaphor traditionally used for this stratagem fits so well that it is chilling to contemplate in its actual reality.

* * *
* *

Let your fortress appear to be empty.

This refers to feigning weakness or inability so as to mislead opponents as to the nature of the threat against them. An example of this is Japan's apparent acceptance of the political-lightweight role, even focusing attention on this itself by public displays of self-excoriation over its supposed passivity in global politics, all the while wielding vast economic power that cannot in reality be separated from political power.

* * *
* *

Employ double agents in your schemes.

Although for some reason this is not formally regarded as employment of double agents, it is well known that powerful Japanese businesses regularly hire Americans formerly employed in critical offices in order to obtain the sensitive information, contacts, and influence necessary to strike deep Japanese roots into the structure of the American economy.

* * *
* *

RESOURCES

The Art of War, by Sun-tzu, translated by Thomas Cleary. (Boston: Shambhala Publications, 1988).

Includes eleven classic commentaries, with Taoist introductory material. Also available, abridged, in pocketbook and audiotape formats.

The Book of Five Rings, by Miyamoto Musashi, translated by Thomas Cleary (Boston: Shambhala Publications, 1993).

A classic on the practice of confrontation and victory, written by the famed seventeenth century duelist and undefeated samurai. Also included is Yagyu Munenori's *Book of Family Traditions on the Art of War,* which emphasizes the spiritual and ethical dimensions of the way of the warrior.

The Japanese Art of War, by Thomas Cleary (Boston: Shambhala Publications, 1991).

An account of the distinctive peculiarities of martial/strategic traditions in Japan as they developed under the prolonged domination of the military caste.

Mastering the Art of War, by Zhuge Liang and Liu Ji, translated and edited by Thomas Cleary (Boston: Shambhala Publications, 1989).

Writings on the martial tradition of Sun-tzu by two of the greatest strategist generals in Chinese history, Zhuge Liang and Liu Ji. Includes discussion of organizational principles as well as war stories illustrating the application of strategic concepts.

Thunder in the Sky: On the Acquisition and Exercise of Power, translated by Thomas Cleary (Boston: Shambhala Publications, 1993).

Presents two secret classics from ancient China on the arts of strategy and leadership, with commentary on the application of these teachings.